Life is Your dance

Notes on Love, Life and Laughter
Illustrated by Karen Hillard Crouch

Especially for

from.

on this day

Published by Lang Books
a division of R.A. Lang Card Co., Ltd.
514 Wells St., Delafield, WI 53018

10 9 8 7 6 5 4 3 2 1

ISBN 0-7412-0434-7

Toll Free # 1-800-967-3399

Dedicated to refreshment of spirit, this notebook is not to be taken too seriously, but perhaps with a cup of tea and a quiet moment. So, go ahead... doodle in it, plant your dreams on its pages, do anything you want!

Special thanks to Baroness Sue MacQueenie and Roxie Kelley for their view of the world. Life is so good!

Best wishes,
Karen

This notebook has been created for every woman who understands the importance of taking care... not just taking care of others, which most of us do by instinct, but also taking care of ourselves.

The spirit of our lives is 'exercised' and strengthened by love and laughter (and we all know what happens when we overlook exercise in our daily routine).

Think of this book as an energizing dance, a reminder to laugh more, love more, and learn more about your beautiful self.

∽ Roxie Kelley

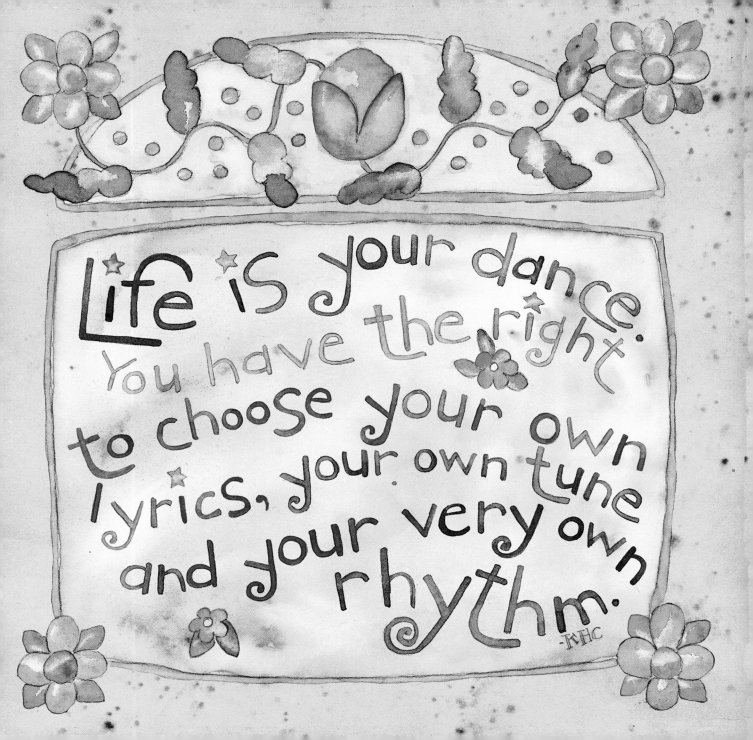

my favorite music

My favorite song lyrics...

a photo from my
beautiful life...

O beautiful human life! Tears come to my eyes as I think of it... So beautiful... the Song shall never be silent, the Dance never still. The Laugh should sound like water which runs forever.

- Jeffries

I still believe that people are really good at heart.
If I look up to the Heavens
I know that it will all come right...
and that peace and tranquility
will return again. -Anne Frank

peaceful places,
peaceful people...

Some of my favorite people...

Beauty
is all
around
us.

I went looking for beauty
and I found...

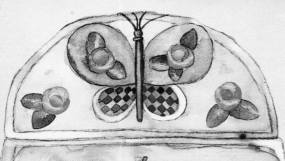

We
struggle
to find life
outside
ourselves,
unaware
that the life
we seek
is
within
US. -Gibran

If I am not I, who will be?

— Thoreau

Glorious loves of my life...

Love, no matter in what way, shape or form it comes to you, is a Glorious thing.

The world is
truly magnificent
...and I'm glad
to be here.

Parts of the world I would like to explore...

One should ask children and birds
what cherries taste like.
— Goethe

A Photo of my favorite little people... (or of anything else that I love.)

Special memories...

Best memories of home.

Things I Love...

my cup runneth over.

Special birthdays
I'll remember...

To lie in a golden field and gaze
upon a hundred butterflies floating
in the summer sunshine is by no
means a waste of time. -KHC

What I
have learned
is mine,
I've had my
thought.
-Thoreau

find your quiet place

new ways to show someone
I care...

Love all the people that You can.

my brightest moments...

I used to be afraid of...

But now...

I'm no longer afraid of storms,
For I am learning to sail my own ship.

~ Louisa May Alcott

Friends must

A
Good friend
Photo
here

Stay together

 I will keep in touch with...

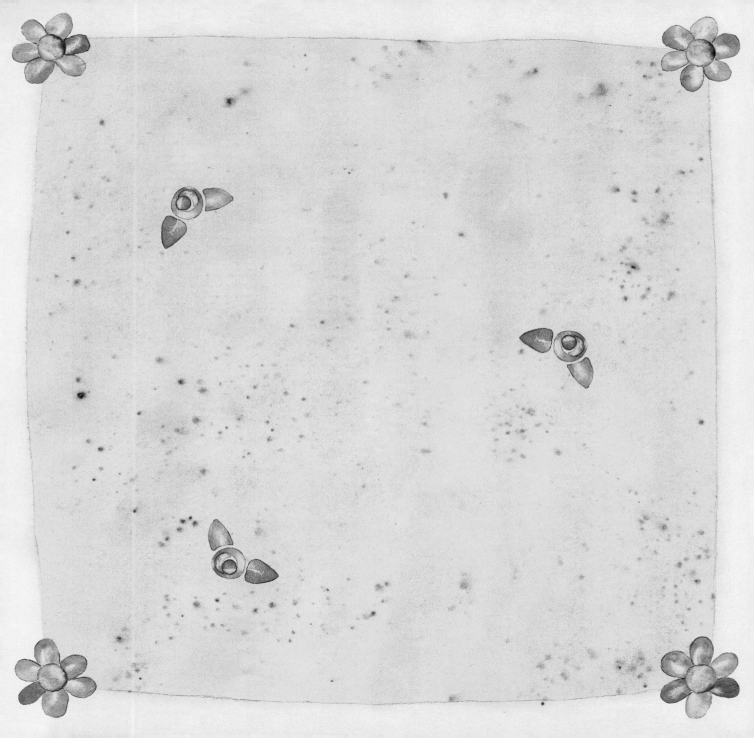

Just think of all
the lovely
things.

Flowers that I like best...

Pansies for thoughts

Girl,
Do not
cook and
scrub and
scour
until you
have no
time left
to plant
a tree or vine or flower.
-unknown

Blessed are we
who can Laugh at ourselves,
for we shall never cease
to be amused. -Unknown

The smartest thing
I ever said
to myself...

Sometimes
the best conversation
I have is with myself.

-KHC

Someday I'll be a Masterpiece,
as for now,
I'm a work in progress.
-KHC

There's only one YOU,

Let your true colors shine through.

Stuff I like about myself...

Laugh
a lot

...even
the
flowers
are
dancing.

more
treasured memories...

I get up.
I walk.
I fall
down.

Meanwhile,
I keep
dancing.

-Hillel

place
photo
here

Remember... every one of those billions of Stars is good for a Wish.

-KHC

My wishes...

always keep at least five kindred companions ...one to encourage, one to keep you humble & three for socializing.

-KHC

If Heaven
has a
Scent,
I'm sure
it's
Gardenia.

adieu...